WHEN WILL WE EVER LEARN

Robert Newbrook

AuthorHouse™
1663 Liberty Drive
Bloomington, IN 47403
www.authorhouse.com
Phone: 1 (800) 839-8640

Published by AuthorHouse 10/06/2015

ISBN: 978-1-5049-4794-7 (sc)
ISBN: 978-1-5049-4793-0 (e)

Print information available on the last page.

Any people depicted in stock imagery provided by Thinkstock are models,
and such images are being used for illustrative purposes only.
Certain stock imagery © Thinkstock.

This book is printed on acid-free paper.

SYNOPSIS

The author relates to the thought processes and deeds of an average person who constantly seeks improvement in the way the human mind and the world works.

Moving through philosophy, belief and relationship phenomena, the book also describes the author's personal experiences of such events as took place in Libya during the 'Six day war' in 1967 between Egypt and Israel, plus an historical incident in Canada involving the American Indian Movement and the FBI in the 1970's.

ABOUT THE AUTHOR.

Bob Newbrook was born on November 16, 1948. He was Christened Robert Michael Newbrook, the third child of a British soldier protestant father and Southern Irish catholic mother. The family traveled extensively to various army postings in the world and he joined the army himself at age 17, serving with the infantry, airborne and military police, terminating his service after 9 years with an 'Exemplary' discharge.

He was married in 1968 and immigrated to Canada with his family in 1975, joining a municipal police force in Alberta where a significant event took place the following year.

Without adhering to any particular religion or realizing exactly what he was seeking, he became interested in Buddhism by coincidence late in life.

AN INCIDENTAL BUDDHIST

*"We cannot solve our problems with the same kind of
thinking which created them in the first place."*
Albert Einstein.

We don't control our thoughts and feelings; they control us. The mind makes us right and others wrong and has us mesmerized; it's a necessary servant but a deadly master. We're frequently dominated by negative thoughts and we'll sacrifice anything to be right, especially in our relationships. Just as our past behavior has conditioned the present, so will our conduct today affect the future and it's a well-established fact of science and nature that for every action, sooner or later there is an equal and opposite reaction. Karma is a natural force like gravity which we can never defy, try as we will.

One bright sunny morning in May of 2011, I was riding my motorbike along a country road in Surrey, British Columbia, Canada, which I had never taken before. I came across a short gravel road which was an entrance to a large acreage surrounded by trees with a sign at the gate written in what I presumed to be the Korean language. It was obviously private property but nevertheless I drove in to look around without really knowing why. There was a house straight ahead and I saw a beautiful temple on a slight hill about two hundred yards away to my right. I met a Korean monk named Tae Ung Sunim and a woman named Sung (pronounced 'Song'), both of whom were dressed in the simple grey clothing of Buddhists and I was invited into the temple. I soon discovered that everyone is welcome regardless of their religion which they are never asked to change. Self-modesty and compassion is the simple essence of Buddhism.

A dog was kept on the premises tied to a kennel near another house and barked constantly. I mentioned that I was a former dog trainer and handler with the British Military Police in my younger days and would be happy to visit a couple of times each week to work with the dog, a female Golden Retriever, on obedience training, exercise and so forth. Sung spoke quite good English and translated for the monk who gratefully accepted.

I arrived at the temple about 7am next morning and found the dog, named May, to be friendly and eager; my life was to change from that point on. As I began my new adventure I watched as Sung and several other women would assist the monk by doing household chores and tending the vegetable gardens and greenhouses on the property. They worked hard as self-sufficient vegetarians and I would occasionally help out while the dog roamed free on the acreage which was a new experience for her; she was so easy to train. At the time Sung was studying Buddhism in the way of a nun but never actually became one….

I'm self-employed so my time is my own. It transpired that I went to the temple around 7 am every morning for most of that year and found that the monk and usually the women would enter the temple at 4am every day to pray and chant for one hour before having breakfast and beginning their chores. On Sundays at 11am every week a large gathering of Korean Buddhist people came to the temple to pray and listen to the monk speak and afterwards have lunch together in a large kitchen area in the main house. I would sometimes stand at the back of the temple during the service, mostly just to feel the energy as I spoke no Korean. On one particular Sunday after about six months the monk spoke to the people in the temple and awarded me the Buddhist name of 'Bo Myung' (meaning brightness or light; to help others). I had no idea about his intention and had just become a Buddhist. It was quite an honor.

I was divorced for about 15 years at the time after 30 years of what was for the most part a good marriage and hadn't met another potential partner since. Anyway, one rainy morning I arrived at the temple about 5 am just as the praying was ending, my intent being to try and meet Sung as she left the temple before she went back to the house but without the monk seeing me. I was afraid that he would question my intentions toward her so (a guilty conscience on my part, methinks) so I parked my car outside the locked rear gate. A high fence surrounds the property and I had to climb to the top of a concrete pillar supporting the gate to get in. It was wet and I slipped, falling into the thorny brambles on the other side. Soaked, scratched and covered in mud I scrambled out of the blackberry bushes while looking around for my eye glasses which I had lost in the fall (I found them later when I took the dog walking in the area). I then crept into the temple but the only person still inside was Sung's best friend, Mina, who speaks very good English. She regarded me with a look of horror at my appearance, asked what had happened and laughed when I explained, saying that I was crazy (I think she was probably right).

A few days later I was sitting outside at a picnic table near the main house drinking tea with Sung and the monk when he said something to her. She told me that he asked why I still visit the temple every morning after so long as I was the only western person among so many Korean people there. I replied that I really enjoyed my time with the dog on their beautiful property, learning about Buddhism and helping with the vegetable gardens and greenhouses. He stood up, mumbled something and walked away laughing. Sung put her hand over her mouth and looked at me, saying "He sees your eyes and said that you come here for me."

I've often wondered if he'd found out about the rear gate incident.

One day I found Sung working alone in one of the greenhouses and she asked what it was that I wanted of her. "To spend the rest of my life with you" I replied without thinking. She said I would have to wait while she considered her fate and I told her I would never give up.

About a week later she said that she would accept her fate, whatever it was to be (I think she had consulted the monk about her dilemma, which was a good thing). Anyway, we've been together now for over four years and I'm still not sure what happened.

I've since learned from Sung that love can be confused with control and unfounded jealousy. Difficult as it may be, an old truism is that if we love someone we must allow them their freedom. If they choose to stay with us then we belong together. If not, then we never did.

Saying goodbye to Tae Ung Sunim (wearing sunglasses) at the airport in Vancouver awaiting his return to Korea.

BELIEF

Religion probably first arose in the attempt to bring love and kindness to each other and it shouldn't be about hatred or trying to convert others to our own belief system; it's an ongoing conflict. What if all religions were to come together and welcome each other, regardless of race or ethnicity, with the common purpose of ending man's inhumanity to man which brings so much suffering to our world? Science and technology cannot replace the age-old spiritual values of love and compassion which is our only hope for survival; burying our heads in the sand won't change anything and this train is going to end up where it's heading unless we humans change our ways. The young generation is the world's only hope, beginning with simple individual acts of kindness which will inevitably spread and become infectious. I remember the movie 'Pay it forward'.

I was recently asked by a woman if the emblem on the finger ring I was wearing was a Nazi Swastika. "No and yes", I answered and explained that the original 'Swastika' was an ancient Hindu emblem of compassion in the Sanskrit language thousands of years before the advent of Nazis. When Adolf Hitler came to power prior to the second world-war, bent on racial purity and discrimination he reversed and tilted the appearance of this symbol to represent their self-righteous hatred, mostly of Jewish people.

I took a sheet of paper from my portfolio and drew the following diagram, explaining that the correct German word for the Nazi emblem is 'hakenkreutz', (haken meaning hooks, and 'kruetz' meaning cross). I hadn't been aware of these facts until I accidentally became a Buddhist, saw the symbol, researched its true origin and had the ring custom made, knowing that its true history is not common knowledge and most people would automatically come to the wrong conclusion through no fault of their own.

BUDDHIST

COMPASSION

NAZI

HATRED

The ring

INTROSPECTION

Impoverishment comes from wanting more, such as material possessions and wealth, yet the more we get the less content we are; we remain in a constant state of dissatisfaction. More *is* less, and I speak from personal experience.

"There are those who enter the world in such poverty that they are deprived of both the means and the motivation to improve their lot. Unless they can be touched with the spark which ignites the spirit of individual enterprise and determination, they will only sink into apathy, degradation and despair. It is for us, who are more fortunate, to provide that spark". His Royal Highness, the Aga Khan.

Going up against life may look like suicide but in reality, *not* going up against life is suicide; slow suicide. To overcome the fear of something, experience that fear and so expand. A true friend is not the person who offers you comfort and refuge, encouraging your old self to survive. Rather, it is someone who will challenge and encourage you in the face of risk and adversity when others become uncomfortable and leave.

Placing too high a value on comfort and safety, dealing only with the familiar, prevents us from realizing the true joy of living and life gets more and more stuck; we seek problems for variety. An experiment was once carried out where a monkey put his hand through a little hole in a transparent plastic wall to reach a treat on the other side. Once he had the treat in his fist, of course, he couldn't pull it back out through the hole. The monkey became hysterical but would not let go. What treat do we get out of holding on to the past? We say we're trying to let go, but we don't actually do it. We dwell on and relive the past constantly, repeating the same old patterns. Perhaps it's a form of being right?

The past is dead; bury it. (Advice which I could well use myself).

The higher our ideals, the more prone we are to self-judgment and the lower our self-worth. The more harshly we judge ourselves the more we judge others and attract criticism, especially from our parents, and in turn pass judgment on others such as our children. Being attached to our opinions and beliefs is not only restricting, it is *the* issue in life. It's our own attitude which determines the response we get from others.

The most devastating denial of freedom is that we are taught from the beginning, not to be philosophical and question everything, but to believe. True philosophy is the willingness to float freely between issues and examine the truth which underlies our beliefs. Speaking of Jesus Christ as an historical figure, he is reputed to have said that the truth shall set you free (i.e. telling the truth as opposed to the edited version). When we have the courage to tell the truth as it is, interesting things begin to happen; the world becomes a different place.

Be the truth; don't use it for something.

"They must find it difficult……………

Those who have taken authority as the truth – rather than truth as the authority."

G. Massey - Eyptologist. From 'Zeitgeist – The Movie'.

It's wise for us to observe the world of our mind and draw the distinction between good and harmful thinking. With constant practice we can learn to foster a beneficial state of mind and detach ourselves from bad emotions which cause harm to ourselves and others.

Ever notice how two people can have opposite opinions about the same thing, yet neither is lying? We all have opinions but making ourselves right and others wrong only serves to destroy relationships on both a personal and global level. The problem is that we believe our opinion is *the truth* as opposed to realizing that it's just our interpretation, which can change.

The drive to enter politics comes from ego, which is one of the mind's greatest weapons, and war is an extension of politics. Most of us long for peace, love and security and each individual has a responsibility to help shape institutions and serve the needs of the world through universal concern. It seems that half the world is once again immersed in the madness of hatred and killing and another world war is in the offing. If it escalates to a nuclear holocaust, which could easily happen, there will be no victors because there will be no survivors. This threat is very real and it seems that we're prepared, not only to kill each other for our religious and political beliefs, but to destroy this beautiful Earth in the process.

Ironically, the most serious problems emanate from industrially and scientifically advanced societies where unprecedented literacy continues to foster more efficient ways of slaughtering increasing numbers of people whom we have never met nor have done us harm. With all our 'progress' we have not only failed to achieve world peace and reduce suffering but have fostered imminent disastrous consequences for humanity. We ignore this at our peril.

A self-centered approach to life and continuing to inflict suffering on others doesn't make us happy for long. Globalization and the miracle of modern communications and international trade mean that the world is rapidly becoming smaller and more interdependent. We need one another more than ever before. One nation's problems cannot be solved by that nation alone. A universal responsibility to world problems is the only sound basis for world peace and we can begin via the United Nations. We are so closely interconnected these days and without an understanding that we are all one people, the world as we know it cannot last.

It's self-defeating to pursue our own happiness without considering other members of our global family, something the late Native American Indian and successful actor Chief Dan George tried to impart. It starts with us by developing a kind heart, compassion for all living beings and respect for our world with everything in it.

AWAKENING

One morning about a year ago I had a business meeting scheduled in Vancouver and decided to take a Surrey City Transit bus number 337 from the stop right outside my home to catch the 'Sky Train' rapid transit system for the first time ever, instead of facing the slow heavy traffic in my car during rush hour (why it's called 'rush hour' is beyond me; it should be 'slush' hour). Not only did it turn out to be much faster but was a life changing experience and provided the incentive for me to write this book.

The bus was full of mostly young people from various Asian countries and, presumably, they were either students or on their way to work. The energy was buzzing that morning with everyone talking and laughing together, mostly in the English language, and I must say that I felt a twinge of racism about how our immigration laws have become so slack here in Western Canada. I suddenly felt ashamed, considering that I too am an immigrant having landed in Canada with my family in 1975 from England. My hypocrisy hit me like a freight train something which I'd experienced before (I'll explain later). "What if the whole world could be like this?" I thought. Unconditional acceptance of each other just as these industrious and good natured people were showing by their example. It was as though there no were no differences between them, which there aren't, other than skin color and language perhaps.

I had visited, lived or served in thirteen countries during my lifetime, including the nine years I spent with the British armed forces. I've seen conflict first-hand so why my thoughts and emotions on the bus that morning? I now see that the proverbial 'melting pot' of so many different races and ethnic groups occupying the same proximity in Surrey, BC, Canada, is the best experiment to end racial prejudice in the world today and I'm proud as a white European to be part of it. I also remember thinking what a difference it would make if all progressive countries taught a universal sign language to children in school starting from grade 1 to graduation. Most of the world could then eventually communicate naturally with each other from childhood (provided, of course, that we could see each other's hands and faces).

BACK TO 1967

Me.

Where have all the flowers gone. Young girls picked them…..
Where have all the young girls gone. Gone to young men…..
Where have all the young men gone. Gone to soldier and graveyards…..
The graveyards went to flower; where have all the flowers gone?
From a song by Pete Seeger.

"When *Sin* claps his broad wings over the battle and sails rejoicing in the flood of death;

When souls are torn to everlasting fire and fiends of hell rejoice upon the slain, who can stand? Who has caused this? Who can answer at the throne of God?

Kings and the leaders of the land have done it. Hear it not, Heaven? **Thy ministers have done it.**" From a poem by William Blake.

My father was a British protestant soldier. He was sent to Southern Ireland in the days when England sought to make the country part of Great Britain where he met and married my very catholic Irish mother (you should have seen the fights in our house as I was growing up). He was posted to Egypt at my age of three accompanied by our family and later we were sent to Cyprus during the Greek EOKA terrorist and Turkey crisis, both of which sought to take ownership of the country. In those days education for children traveling with parents of the armed forces was mostly taught in makeshift schools by volunteer housewives. From there we went to Germany and eventually returned to England at my age of 13 where I attended a regular secondary school; I was a terrible student. I left at age 15 and worked at menial jobs for two years until my 17th birthday when I joined the British army myself.

I remember an incident during basic training when I was struggling with the erection of my little tent when the sergeant came up behind me;

"**Newbrook, you idiot**" (He reminded me of my father). "**That tent's inside out**"

"That's OK Sarge", I replied. "I'll sleep on the outside."

He hit me.

On completion of my training I was first posted to West Germany when, on 22 May 1967, Nasser of Egypt blockaded Israel's southern port of Eilat and the Gulf of Aqabe which was vital for cargo shipments and most of Israel's oil imports. It was internationally regarded as an act of war and the combined forces of Egypt, Jordan and Syria with the support of other Arabic countries crossed the Sinai desert, amassing at Israel's border with the intent of wiping the country off the map, once and for all. (I've never been able to understand why so much hatred has been directed toward the Jewish people for so long. Political and religious explanations make no sense to me).

Full scale battles began on June 5 and the conflict became known as the 'Six Day War' because that's how long it took for Israel to finish what Egypt et al had started. As a result of the disastrous outcome of the Arab countries aggression toward Israel we were sent to Libya to engage in 'internal security duties' and made our way to Benghazi where riots and violence had ensued. On arrival we learned that the British and U.S. embassy compounds had been attacked and burned; consequently we took over an old airfield and gathered together many European civilians for shelter in disused aircraft hangars and other buildings, receiving adequate supplies of food and bedding on their behalf from echelon.

When we weren't in the streets we were on constant standby and during one particular skirmish we came across a small British armored car which was under gunfire. The officer was dead and the driver injured and unable to escape but we fought back the insurgents and managed to get him to the medics for treatment. *(This was a particularly memorable incident as about 20 years later I met an Irishman, who was a bus driver at the time, in a pub on Christmas Eve in Tsawwassen, BC, Canada. We struck up a conversation and he mentioned that he had been in Libya during the six day war with an armoured car regiment. He started to relate how his vehicle was attacked….I finished the story for him. It turned out that he was the armored car driver whom we had rescued. After staring at each other for an eternity, it seemed, he hugged the stuffing out of me and forbade that I even try to buy a drink on that coincidental Christmas Eve).* I lost his phone number and never heard from him again but what a coincidence.

A NEW DIRECTION

After our return to Germany from Libya I met Maria, a Polish/German immigrant girl and married her a year later when I was twenty years of age and she seventeen. In 1970 I was posted to Malta with my new wife where we had our first child. Whilst there I was attached to the Corps of Royal Military Police (RMP) and trained as a guard dog handler, ultimately transferring to the Corps itself and returning to England with my family for military and civilian police law education in 1971. On completion I was posted to 112 Provost Company RMP in Osnabruck, Germany where I had first met my wife. She was once again close to her family and we had two more children.

In 1973 I was sent to Medicine Hat, Alberta, Canada unaccompanied by my family to work with the city police for 4 months owing to the large contingency of British soldiers who were stationed at the nearby heavy armour live firing training range in Suffield. I was so impressed with the country that upon returning to my unit I started the application process for immigration but was turned down. I applied a second time but was again refused so I took some leave of absence and jumped on a plane back to Medicine Hat. I obtained three written offers of employment, sponsorship from a police friend and opened a bank account. On my third application I was granted an interview at the Canadian Immigration office.

"So you're Mr. Newbrook" the gentleman said as I entered his office. I asked what the specific reasons were that my applications were being declined as I'd never had so much as a speeding ticket. He told me that trades people were being given priority as "they could get police officers anywhere in Canada". Then looking down he mumbled something and stamped a piece of paper.

That was it. In 1975 I immigrated to Canada and joined the Hinton Police Department in the beautiful Rocky Mountains of Alberta where an international event involving the FBI was to happen the following year.

SENIOR CONSTABLES COURSE NO. 15,
"K" DIV. EDMONTON, ALTA. 2-11 MAR 76.

BACK   Csts. M. CHISLETT, M.T. McMAHON, P.C. FULLBRANDT, T.A. LAMOND, J.C. OMAN,
ROW: Csts. W.N. HINDLE, J.V.T. PLAMONDEN, D.H. MALWAS, R.S. GUTHRIE, G.A. POTTRUFF.

CENTRE Csts. D.G. SCHAEFER, P. CHAPUT, B.J. PERCIVAL, G.G.J. LEGAULT, H.W. RASMUSSEN,
ROW: Csts. P.G. DOBSON, C.J.E. LEE, J.W. RADVAK, P.S. KACHOR, A.J. CAMERON.

FRONT Csts. R. NEWBROOK, D.B. BEST, Cpl. R.F. CROY, Supt. J.B. THORNE, Cst. F.S. CREASER,
ROW: Cst. R.J. METTLEWSKY.

One day whilst on routine duty patrolling in a large park area I was chasing a pickup truck for a suspected alcohol violation by the occupants along a gravel road, not thinking that somewhere up ahead was an open railway crossing without barriers. I was having difficulty seeing through all the dust being churned up by the speeding vehicle when I heard a sudden loud train whistle and 'BANG'; I was hit by a freight train. It was over in seconds and I found myself upside down in the new police car beside the tracks and managed to crawl out through the driver's side broken window. The train's braking and screeching wheels finally brought it to a halt and eventually three engineers came running down the railroad toward me. One of them panted "Are you OK?" I had a few scratches and a little bleeding but was otherwise fine. "Yes, thanks", I replied. He stared at me and said, loudly "You should be dead." He then told me that there had been two fatalities at that very crossing in the years before my arrival in town; one the driver of a mobile crane and the other the driver of a pickup truck.

I contacted the police office on my hand-held radio and asked the stenographer to fetch the chief constable, 'Dodger' Clarke. A few minutes later I heard his voice.

"Hi Bob. What's happening?"
"I just got hit by a train, Chief."
He laughed and asked again what I wanted as he was busy.
"I just got hit by a train, Chief."
Silence.
"Chief? You still there?"
"How's the new police car Bob?"
"Oh, I'm fine thanks, Chief, Just a few scratches and….."
"How's the new police car, Bob?"

About fifteen minutes later another police car came speeding down the gravel road from the direction of town. The chief got out, wearing his smart looking uniform as usual, took in the sight of what was left of the police car, the stationary freight train, me and the engineers standing around. A few days later a picture of that very scene, with the chief in the process of throwing his hat to the ground, appeared on the front page of the local newspaper together with a newly erected professional-looking sign;

'STOP'
Police Only

On February 5th of 1976 I commenced duty at 8am when my shift partner George Scullion told me that we had received information about a Native American Lakota Sioux Indian man who was being hunted by the FBI for murdering two of their special agents on 26 June the previous year. He was suspected of being somewhere in Western Canada, possibly at a First Nations Indian reserve north of Edmonton. I happened to know of a remote traditional Native Indian settlement called 'Chief Smallboy's Camp' which was located in the foothills about a two hour drive from Hinton over rugged trails through heavy forest. Chief Robert Smallboy and Shaman Lazarus Roan had many years before founded the encampment on 'Crown land' which they claimed belonged to the First Nations. I know nothing of the politics involved but the Native people continue to live there in peace to this day.

We decided to check it out just for the sake of it. Another officer, Ross Lewis, was finishing the midnight shift and having breakfast at a local restaurant. We contacted him by radio and he agreed to remain on duty until our return; probably around noon. We took an unmarked Chevy Suburban vehicle belonging to the municipality and drove up to the camp in light snow but otherwise good weather conditions.

On arrival at the camp, which was comprised of about eight well-built houses and a few other buildings, we saw three Native men standing together near a building which I later discovered to be the old schoolhouse. They took little notice of our vehicle until we got out and approached them on foot in police uniform. George remained behind me with the shotgun and after a short conversation with one of the three, a slim man with braids who said his name was Black Horse, I turned to question the other two. One was visibly uncomfortable, had no identification and was subsequently detained under suspicion of being Leonard Peltier, the most wanted man in FBI history. We drove him to the Hinton police jail where he was handed over the following morning to the federal RCMP. Later that afternoon two more uniformed officers arrived with Black Horse in custody. He was laughing and joking with the officers who requested that we hold him in our jail overnight. They picked him up the following morning and he was never heard of again.

I think there is a lot of missing information which could be learned from Black Horse about the gunfight on Pine Ridge. It turns out that his real name is Frank Deluca and he was not of Native American descent but Italian; a 'wannabe' Indian. Given that he had aided and abetted the escape of the FBI's most wanted man ever it's interesting that he disappeared apparently without charges or trace. Was he present at the shootout on Pine Ridge? If so, what did he see and what role did he take? I also never found out what happened to the third person in camp that day whose name was ostensibly Ron Janvier or Ron Blackman, nor what his part in the ordeal was. Nevertheless, Leonard was extradited to the U.S. for trial, found guilty of the murders of FBI Special Agents Ron Williams and Jack Coler and sentenced to 2 consecutive life terms without parole.

FULL CIRCLE

I had never suspected anything untoward in the case nor carried out any further research but 23 years later in 1999, long after I had left the police force, I saw by coincidence a movie documentary by the actor Robert Redford entitled 'Incident at Oglala' which exposed the extensive fabrication of evidence by the FBI against Peltier. Consequently I returned to Hinton and re-visited Smallboy's camp in the company of an acquaintance from my police days, a Cree Indian named Ken Desjarlais. Nobody knew in advance of my visit and there were no telephones or cell phones in camp at that time. I met first with long-term resident Harvey Rain in the presence of his wife Lorraine Smallboy, who is the granddaughter of the camp's founder Robert Smallboy. They related to me that three men, all of whom they presumed were Native, had arrived at camp early in 1976 and had rarely communicated with the residents other than to mention they were travelling and writing a book about traditional Native settlements. They slept in the schoolhouse and would tidy away their belongings before the few children in camp came to school each day.

One morning a few days after the three men's arrival, Harvey and Lorraine related how they were leaving camp for Hinton in their vehicle to buy groceries and saw one of the three visitors standing by the side of the road at the exit. The man asked for a ride into town, to which they agreed, but didn't know the person's name and nor did they ask. As they continued along the road around the first bend they were stopped at a road block of heavily armed police who took the passenger from their vehicle and after some brief questioning waived them on. (I think the passenger may have been Blackhorse).

I also interviewed the schoolteacher, whose last name is Roan, as well as two other men named Rattlesnake and Yellow Bird who were teenaged students at the time and were witnesses to what happened in the schoolhouse that same morning. The schoolteacher told me that he had entered the classroom about 10am and saw one of the individuals, whom he assumed was Peltier, sitting at a table praying quietly. Shortly afterwards a tall white man in civilian clothing entered the room, held a gun to the individual's head, told him he was under arrest, placed handcuffs on the suspect's wrists and took him outside. At this point I became confused as it didn't coincide with what I knew but it was clear to me that these people had no apparent reason to make up stories. I could only conclude that, after Peltier was taken from the Hinton police office by the RCMP, they returned to Smallboy's camp to apprehend Blackhorse for the record and stage Leonard's arrest in front of witnesses for 'continuity of evidence'.

FURTHER RESEARCH

Leonard Peltier was born on September 12, 1944, at Grande Forks, North Dakota. His maternal grandmother was a full blood Sioux and his father ¾ Ojibwa and ¼ French. In 1968, the American Indian Movement (AIM) was formed as a direct result of the relocation of bewildered Indians into the cities facing open racism and discrimination, the conflict over fishing rights, continuing land transgressions by corporate interests and the longstanding policies of government in dealing with Native people. Leonard became an active leader of AIM and faced increasing malicious persecution by the FBI.

Through the use of sophisticated NASA satellite technology, the National Uranium Resource Evaluation Program of the U.S. Geological Survey had located significant uranium deposits in the northwest corner of the Pine Ridge Reservation in an area called Sheep Mountain. Multinational energy corporations, such as Kerr-McGee, wanted that uranium but, once again, the Indians were in the way. In 1973 a standoff at Wounded Knee between traditional Natives and the U.S. army together with police authorities resulted in the deaths of two Indians. Over the following two years, a government financed, FBI armed and trained group of vigilante militants known as the 'Guardians Of the Oglala Nation' (GOON), mostly of mixed blood and led by tribal chairman Dick Wilson, conducted a reign of terror and oppression against the Lakota people of Pine Ridge. Road blocks were erected throughout the reservation and the constant harassment included assaults, drive by shootings and executions. During the time between the standoff at Wounded Knee in 1973 and the deaths of the FBI Special Agents in 1975, over 60 murders on the reservation were officially recorded although not one was ever investigated by the authorities.

The FBI created a national campaign against the AIM movement within their secret counterintelligence program (COINTELPRO) and established itself on Native land as a paramilitary force with all other government agents subject to FBI control. In 1975, a buildup of FBI SWAT, GOONS and other police took place on Pine Ridge. The Lakota had asked AIM for help and warriors set up an encampment on the private property of the Jumping Bull family near the village of Oglala on the Pine Ridge reservation.

Around this time Dick Wilson was in Washington, illegally signing away that part of the Pine Ridge reserve containing uranium deposits. On June 26, 1975, two FBI Special Agents, Ron Williams and Jack Coler, drove onto the private property of Jumping Bull in pursuit of a red truck containing a Native man named Jimmy Eagle, who was alleged to have stolen a pair of used boots after a fight. Hardly an FBI mandate, it was the reason given for gaining access to sovereign lands and private property under the 'lawful procedure of continuous pursuit' provisions. Given the previous history of violence and killing on the reservation, this could easily have been perceived by the occupants as another offensive and, although no one is sure of exactly what happened, both agents and one Native, Joe Killsright Stuntz, were killed in the ensuing gunfight.

A large contingent of police authorities, who just happened to be in close proximity at the time, swarmed the property within minutes and began firing indiscriminately at the AIM members and fleeing residents, including women, children and elders. Two Native men, Dino Butler and Bob Robideau, were subsequently arrested and brought to trial in Cedar Rapids, Iowa. The defense was allowed to present evidence of the circumstances of the oppressive tactics by the GOONS leading up to the firefight, and both men were found not guilty by an all-white jury on the basis of self defense. Leonard Peltier, who had also been present during the incident, escaped and was detained at Chief Smallboy's camp near Hinton, Alberta, Canada in February,

1976. He was subsequently extradited to the United States based on suborned and fabricated evidence provided by the FBI.

The Canadian Court which approved the extradition was presented with an affidavit by a Native woman named Myrtle Poor Bear, which stated that she was Peltier's girlfriend and had witnessed him kill the agents. It was subsequently ascertained that she had been subjected to abusive tactics by FBI agents to coerce the statement from her, that she had a history of mental illness, had never met Peltier and was not present at the scene at the time of the gunfight.

At trial, Ms. Poor Bear attempted to recant her evidence citing scare tactics used by the FBI, such as showing her photos of the corpse of a Native woman named Anna Mae Aquash with the hands cut off. She said the agents had told her that the same would happen to her if she didn't co-operate and sign the affidavit. However, her testimony was barred on the basis of mental incompetence, although the original document was accepted and allowed to stand.

Critical ballistic information was withheld from the defense team. Specifically, a written report by Evan Hodge, an FBI ballistics expert, showed that in October of 1975 he had conducted an extractor mark test on the .223 bullet shell casings allegedly recovered near the agent's vehicles and found that none matched the AR-15 rifle belonging to Peltier. During the trial, however, Hodge testified that he had performed a test on the same casings in February 1976 and had found them to match Peltier's gun. Also, he stated that a firing pin test is far more conclusive than a shell casing test, but could not be performed owing to damage to the weapon. However, the documents showed that the October 1975 ballistic testing had, in fact, included the more precise firing pin test and that the results were negative. At trial, defense counsel was not aware of this conflicting information and Hodge perjured himself.

There are several thousand FBI documents still being withheld in direct violation of Leonard Peltier's rights to a fair hearing. Mr. Warren Allmand, then Solicitor General of Canada, wrote in consequence: "It was only after the extradition and Peltier's return to the United States when we learned that the affidavit submitted to the Canadian court was false, and that certain other evidence had been concealed. As a Minister of the Crown at that time, I consider myself and the Canadian Government to have been misled by the authorities of the American Government. This is not the treatment one expects between friendly sovereign nations and as a result, I have been pursuing this matter for over 12 years."

August 17, 1992.

<u>Leonard Peltier remains in prison</u>

THE CASE OF JOHN GRAHAM

As a result of my involvement with the Leonard Peltier case I was introduced by Amnesty International in 2004 to John Graham, a Canadian First Nations Tuchone and former AIM warrior. He was alleged by the FBI to have murdered a Mi'kmaq Native woman from Nova Scotia named Anna Mae Aquash, also an AIM member, some six months after the incident at Oglala on Pine Ridge when the two federal agents were killed. That the FBI would arrest an AIM terrorist for killing another AIM terrorist after 32 years was highly suspicious, as none of over 60 murders of traditional native people on Pine Ridge between the time of the AIM/US standoff at Wounded Knee in 1973 and the killing of the agents on Pine Ridge in 1975 was ever investigated by US authorities.

Apparently, rumors of Anna Mae's supposed sexual indiscretions among the Lakota men on the reservation and being an FBI informant were common place on the reservation and a function of the FBI's counter intelligence program (COINTELPRO), causing ill will toward her by the tribal women and AIM members.

FBI documents which I subsequently read state that the frozen body of a Native woman was found on private land near Wanblee, South Dakota on February 24, 1976 by the owner of the property, Roger Amiotte. A pathologist for the Bureau of Indian Affairs (BIA), Dr. W.O. Brown, was appointed by the FBI to perform an autopsy the following day which included, by his statement "the removal of the brain from the body" and the cause of death was determined as exposure. The hands were severed and sent to FBI headquarters, presumably to match the finger prints with those of Anna Mae which John said had been taken by FBI agent Price a few months earlier according to her. The body was buried anonymously without licence in a pauper's grave.

Lawyer Bruce Ellison, who had previously been involved as legal counsel for AIM, ordered the body to be exhumed on March 11, 1976 and another pathologist, Dr. Garry Peterson, carried out a second autopsy and determined the cause of death as a bullet wound to the head, something the FBI pathologist had somehow failed to discover.

Mystery and intrigue have surrounded the case for years. On September 16, 1999, a distant cousin of Anna Mae, Robert Pictou-Branscombe, convened a press conference in which he stated that FBI provocateur Douglass Durham had planted rumors about Anna Mae being an FBI informant. He further alleged that she had been taken to a house on the reservation in South Dakota where she was interrogated by senior AIM members. Branscombe also alleged that she was killed by John Graham but gave no details. The FBI quickly responded by stating that new evidence would be put before a grand jury.

In 2003 a homeless alcoholic Native man named Arlo Looking Cloud was arrested and convicted in court as an accessory in the first degree murder of Anna Mae Aquash and is currently serving a life sentence. He did not testify at his trial and the only evidence against him was a video showing Looking Cloud being interviewed by police who subjected him to leading questions. Shortly before the interview Looking Cloud had visited the murder scene with police officer Bob Ecoffey, ostensibly to re-enact the crime for police evidence. During the interview he agreed with prompts by the police that he saw John Graham take Anna Mae to the grassy embankment below which her body was later found lying in the arroyo and shoot her in the back of the head on December 12, 1975.

In an FBI document entitled "A summary of investigation of the death of Anna Mae Aquash" it is stated that "During the crime scene search, the earth below where Aquash's head had rested was spaded in an effort to obtain physical evidence of which none was located and no earth was removed from the scene. There was no evidence of foul play."

From the beginning of my investigation John had told me that he and Anna Mae were close acquaintances and were in Rapid City attending the trial of Crow Dog, who had been present at the standoff at Wounded Knee, when they heard about the gunfight at Pine Ridge on the radio. He said that they immediately left for the reservation to help the Lakota occupants in any way they could and had separated shortly thereafter. He said that he saw her again later that year when they drove from Denver to a 'safe house' on Pine Ridge, although he couldn't remember who's house it was, where it was or who was inside as it had been thirty years since he was there and didn't know the reservation well.

He also told me that during the journey, Anna Mae had explained to him how agent Price had arrested her while they had been separated and taken photos and finger prints. He said Price had threatened that she would not live out the year unless she named all the AIM warriors who were present at the shootout when the two agents were killed. He added that she was afraid and in hiding from the FBI but had no reason to fear AIM, and that the FBI had also harassed him on various occasions including once in the Yukon where they tried to compel him to cooperate by giving up the names of all the AIM warriors present at the shootout, or be implicated in Anna Mae's death.

In June of 2007 John was arrested in Vancouver, Canada and held in custody for 3 months before being tried and extradited to the US in September of that year. In December of 2010 he was found guilty in state court, Rapid City, South Dakota of felony murder (kidnapping resulting in the murder of the victim by persons unknown) which carries a mandatory life sentence without parole.

According to a 1999 article by the Canadian newspaper *Globe and Mail,* Anna Mae had been staying at Troy Lynn Yellow Wood's house on Pecos Street in Denver for a few weeks when she was taken by John Graham, Arlo Looking Cloud and Theda Clark to South Dakota to be questioned about being an informant. It states; "Yellow Wood said they made it clear that Ms. Aquash was being ordered back to South Dakota. She was unhappy about going. She did not want to go but she also wanted to get things straightened up. She was tired of people making untrue statements about her. The three people left with Aquash after dark. She said she would go to not make trouble for me. She walked out on her own but I don't think she had any choice in the matter"

Candy Hamilton, who was a legal assistant to the Wounded Knee Legal Defence/Offence Committee (WKLDOC), testified at trial that she was working upstairs in the office and saw Anna Mae there, but couldn't do anything about her predicament at the time.

Angie Begay Janis, a woman whom John had never told me about but who, I later found out, he had been living with in Denver during the time when Anna Mae was murdered, testified at his and Looking Cloud's trials. She stated in court that she had visited Troy Lynn Yellow Wood's house in November or December of 1975 because she had received a phone call from Thelma Rios, another traditional Native woman involved with AIM, saying that Anna Mae was an informant and should be taken to South Dakota for questioning.

She said that she told John Graham and her aunt Theda Clark who were inside the house about the call. A dozen or so other traditional Native people were summoned to the house and they all met upstairs in the kitchen to discuss the situation. After about two hours she saw John Graham and Looking Cloud bring Anna Mae up from the basement, where they had been during the meeting, "tied to a board and taken out of the house to a red Ford Pinto hatchback which belonged to Theda".

She went on to testify that John Graham was away for two or three days after this incident before returning but had said nothing about where he had been or what had happened, and she didn't ask.

She never saw Anna Mae Aquash again.

John had stayed in touch with me by phone regularly since first being taken to South Dakota and I visited him in Sioux Falls prison on April 30, 2011. I told him I was going to Pine Ridge to meet the man who had discovered Anna Mae's body, Roger Amiotte. He asked why, as Roger had already testified at his trial and there was nothing to add. I told him I was trying to gather any additional information which might conflict with the prosecution's evidence and thereby create enough doubt for a possible appeal trial jury to acquit him, should he be granted one.

Then, without mentioning that he'd never told me about Angie Begay Janis, I asked him what he felt about her testimony. He said "Anna Mae wasn't tied to a board. That was bullshit. How could she fit into a little Pinto tied to a board with me, Looking Cloud, Theda and George Palfey all inside? Palfey's a big guy. She went of her own free will. We dropped Palfey off somewhere and carried on to the safe house at Pine Ridge."

That statement contradicted everything John had previously told me.

The next day I headed west for Pine Ridge along interstate 90 in a small rented car against the strongest wind I have ever experienced in my life. I saw a large semi-trailer truck on its side near the junction of highway 73 leading south to the reservation, and heard from someone at the gas station about three other trucks having met the same fate.

I met with Roger and his wife Twyla at their home at 9am sharp on Sunday, May 1.

I interviewed him and recorded the conversation with his permission. He was very clear that the body he found in late February of 1976 was that of a Native American person with long hair, but he could not determine what sex it was from his vantage point of about 10 or 15 feet owing to the "sunken facial features." The clothing worn by the body consisted of a black leather car-coat type of jacket and black or dark colored Levi type pants. I mentioned that the record states the body of Anna Mae Aquash was wearing a burgundy jacked and blue jeans, but Roger shrugged it off and said with a laugh that "Somebody must have been color blind". (I'm not yet sure about the significance of this inconsistency).

He did not approach the body any closer for fear of disturbing the scene and immediately drove back to his house about a mile distant to call the police. He agreed that the corpse could have been in that location since December as the weather had been extremely cold during the prior two months but was finally warming up.

Roger then drove me to the murder scene but Twyla would not accompany us because of the spirits there. As he showed me around and explained the sequence of events, he told me something which he'd never spoken of before for fear of reprisal. At the time when he discovered the body he immediately remembered that about two months prior he had taken a drive about 10pm one night to check on his cattle and came across a car stopped in the middle of the road at 90 degrees with the headlights facing the grassy knoll below where he would later find the body. There were four Native Indian people standing beside the car which was a large, dark colored four door sedan. He asked the three young men and one woman if their car had broken down and offered temporary refuge in his nearby home, noticing that they were acting strangely. He drove them back to his house to make coffee and get help by way of calling a tow truck or something.

They stayed at the house for approximately 45 minutes, mostly huddling together across the other side of the living/dining room, speaking in whispers and glancing at Roger. He started to feel a sense of dread and asked if he should call the tribal police to assist but the woman, whom he described as large and bossy, moved to the phone and said "You're not calling anyone."

Finally they requested that he drive them to a house about 12 miles away along a gravel road to the south-west, to which he agreed, but didn't know who was living in the old log building and neither did he ask. He dropped them off and immediately returned home. Early the following morning he drove back to where he had come across the car the previous night but it was gone.

I think Roger had happened upon Theda Clark, John Graham, Looking Cloud and another man, possibly a guide and the owner of the large car, just a few yards from where he would later find Anna Mae's body but I have no proof of that.

So it seems what possibly happened during those heady days on the Pine Ridge Indian reservation in December of 1975 is that Anna Mae Aquash was taken to the Wounded Knee Legal Defence/Offence Committee office in Rapid City by John Graham, Looking Cloud and Theda Clark (since deceased) in her red Ford Pinto and questioned by senior AIM members. Then on December 12 she was driven to the execution site by the same people plus another man, who was possibly a guide and the owner of the large sedan, taken to the small cliff edge, shot in the back of the head and fell about 15 feet to the bottom of the cliff.

She died in the fetal position and her body was found in February 1976 by the owner of the property, Roger Amiotte.

Roger at the murder scene (the fence was erected some years after he had found the body).

FURTHER RESEARCH

No true white person can look at the history of North America and not feel a mix of pride and shame, in particular with respect to the struggle of native people to remain themselves. Some of the following information was taken from the book "In the spirit of Crazy Horse" by the late Peter Matthieson. The remainder is from the examination of FBI documentation under the Freedom of Information Act, other research and my involvement with the detaining of Leonard Peltier.

The following quote is purported to be from the Lakota Sioux war chief Sitting Bull. He would not accept relocation to a reservation and was killed resisting arrest in 1890.

"What treaty that the white man made has the red man broken? Not one.

What treaty that the white man made have they kept? Not one.

When I was a boy, the Sioux owned the world. The sun rose and set on their land; they sent ten thousand men to battle. Where are the warriors today? Who slew them? Where are our lands; who owns them? What white man can say I ever stole his land or a penny of his money? Yet, they say I am a thief. What white woman was ever held captive or insulted by me? Yet, they say I am a bad Indian. What white man has ever seen me drunk? Who has ever come to me hungry and unfed? Who has ever seen me abuse my wife or children? What law have I broken? Is it wrong for me to love my own? Is it wicked for me because my skin is red, because I am Lakota, because I was born where my father died, because I would die for my people and my land?"

In 1835, five white prospectors who entered the old silences of the sacred mountains were attacked by Native Indians; their fate was scrawled in a last note, "All kilt but me". Probably

Erza Kind's small expedition was the first to pursue the sunny glint of gold in the earth and streams of the Black Hills, an isolated ridge of Pine-dark peaks and high blue lakes that rises strangely from the dry plains on what is now the Wyoming-South Dakota border. It has a mystery and power, as if it were a sacred place at the center of the world. It was a place for shelter and hunting deer and birds with sparkling clear water for the Lakota people, where great tribal gatherings would take place for renewal ceremonies such as the sun dance, where one takes the decision to meet one's self.

The first white men to appear from the North and East in the 18th century were tolerated, if not welcomed, by the strong and warlike buffalo people of the plains who were to become known as the Sioux by white people. As the whites increased in numbers, Indians began dying of measles or smallpox which was explained to them by their white visitors as the work of God, clearing the way for his own people in the wilderness. As time progressed, the U.S. cavalry began a policy of setting one tribe against another which, together with the awful plagues, killed thousands of Native people all over the Great Plains.

The onslaught of whites forged muddy trails across the sacred hunting grounds, slaughtering buffalo and elk along the way mainly for the skins to be transported back East for export to Europe and the resulting riches it would bring the white man. That the meat was left to rot while Indians began starving was of no consequence. The U.S. government, eager to adopt a friendship policy permitting safe passage of pioneers and trappers, signed a treaty in 1851 at Fort Laramie. In 1854, Colonel William Harney responded to a bloody skirmish over a Mormon cow by killing more than one hundred warriors and marching the rest into Fort Laramie in chains. Four years later, a party of soldiers reconnoitered the Black Hills.

Red Cloud of the Oglala, the most powerful band of the Lakota Sioux nation, stalked out in the middle of a discussion with the whites about opening up a trail which came to be called

"Thieves Road" by the Indians. He consequently made the statement "The great father sends us presents and wants us to sell him the road, but the white chief comes with soldiers to steal it before the Indian says yes or no! I will talk with you no more. I will go, and I will fight you. As long as I live, I will fight you for the last hunting grounds of my people".

According to the terms of the treaty signed by Red Cloud at Fort Laramie on November 6, 1868, the Indians were guaranteed "Absolute and undisturbed use of the Great Sioux Reservation. No persons…shall ever be permitted to pass over, settle upon or reside in territory described in this article, or without consent of the Indians pass through the same. No treaty for the cession of any portion or part of the reservation herein scribed …shall be of any validity or force… unless executed and signed by at least three-fourths of all the adult male Indians, occupying or interested in the same."

Congress, in its Christian duty, had set forth to 'civilize' the Indian with the trusty mix of guns and bibles. The purpose of the reservation system was to "Reduce the wild beasts to the condition of supplicants for charity." Already white mountain-men and prospectors were passing through the Black Hills without the Indian's consent, and the rumor of 'gold in them thar hills' was confirmed in August 1874 by a reconnaissance expedition led by a jubilant colonel George Custer. In 1873, Custer had been condemned by his superior officer as a cold-blooded, untruthful and unprincipled man, universally disliked by all the officers of his regiment. Custer, on the other hand, depicted the Indian as a "cruel and ferocious wild beast of the desert" and did not deserve to be treated like a human being.

Gold-crazed miners who shot their way into the Black Hills in defiance of the Indian war parties were termed by Sitting Bull in 1875 as "The greedy ones. Their love of possessions is a disease with them. We want no white men here. The Black Hills belong to me. If the whites try to take them, I will fight."

That year, a commission was sent out from Washington to 'treat with the Sioux' for the relinquishment of the Black Hills. Sitting Bull refused to attend, as did Red Cloud and Crazy Horse. Since the Sioux were being 'so unreasonable', President Grant sent General Crook to expedite matters. He was asked, prior to leaving, if it was hard for him to go on yet another Indian campaign, to which he made the famous reply, "Yes, it is hard. But the hardest thing is to go and fight those whom you know are in the right."

The 'hostile' Sioux had now been joined by numerous bands of Cheyenne, Arapaho, Miniconjou and Blackfeet which has been described by historians as the greatest gathering of Indian people ever assembled. A great sun dance was held at Medicine Rocks in what is now Montana, where Sitting Bull stood all day staring into the sun when through his vision he saw the bluecoats falling.

On June 25, 1876, on a windy ridge known as Little Big Horn in South Dakota, General Custer, in his greed and haste for the glory, ignored orders to wait for re-enforcements and led a column of two hundred pony soldiers to their deaths.

On December 29, 1890, more than two hundred Lakota Sioux women, children and men were slaughtered by the 7th cavalry at Wounded Knee, South Dakota on what is today the Pine Ridge Indian Reservation. The regiment received twenty congressional medals of honour from a grateful government.

PHILOSOPHY

Do not feel abandoned; I am always with you…
Listen to me in the feelings of your heart…

I will not leave you. I cannot leave you for you are My creation, My son, My daughter, My purpose and My….Self…

(From the book 'Conversations with God' by Neale Donald Walsch).

What is death for a caterpillar is new life for a butterfly. In order to grow we must sometimes leave the old behind and move on to new pastures. A farewell is necessary before we can meet again, and meeting again is certain for those who are truly friends.

Death symbols incompletion; failure to do what we set out for. What did we set out for? When someone close to us dies, we feel incomplete. They show up as missing in more places than just their body. Whatever is missing in our relationships should be communicated while we're together. It will be we who are stuck with it and no-one else.

Closed eyes cannot see the white roses…
Life is the time we can help them,
So give them the flowers now
Leigh M. Hodges

Who is responsible for how our life goes? I presume that for people with cancer, life is real, a deadline pressed up against their faces. The present moment really counts. For those of us who don't have life pressed up against our faces, things are just 'ho-hum; this isn't it – there must be more'.

We find something in the other person in our lives which we don't like and punish them for it. Negative expression destroys but positive expression uplifts. When we criticize we are not expressing feelings, but judgment. Consider your power to uplift or destroy the feelings of another person. The only constant is change, and in relationships we cause damage when we resist change. I learned that the hard way. Are we prepared to accept change instead of building a case against the other person?

Getting others to do what we want by making them feel guilty isn't love; it's creative nastiness. On the other hand, being nice to everyone is devastating because no-one really knows where they stand with you.

Assuming too much responsibility for others and giving unwanted help disempowers them and debilitates us. On the other hand, helping someone to find the key to a problem is empowering for them. Give as much help as is needed and no more. When we establish our boundaries we can take control of what is our responsibility and let go of what is not. In order to live free and happy we must sacrifice false responsibility; not an easy sacrifice.

How is it that relationships often emphasize the emptiness we feel? If the other person has the power to give us happiness, they also have the power to take it away. It isn't their job to make us happy; it's up to us to bring our own well-being to the relationship. Is it fair to expect someone to meet all of our needs? Can we meet all of theirs? Why do we set it up so that people can't get close to us and then resent them for it? Why do we choose to be 'stuck' in a relationship looking elsewhere for the person we are already with and it takes some kind of crisis to wake us up?

I remember seeing a movie with Gene Hackman where he was acting the part of a soldier lost in enemy territory. He was talking on the radio to an aircraft pilot who was trying to locate and rescue him and was saying that when he was back in the U.S. and safe with his wife, all he could ever think about was other women. Now that he was alone and in mortal danger, all he could think about was his wife.

Funny how the mind works.

Bob Newbrook
September, 2015

Printed in the United States
By Bookmasters